Jerry Pallotta's
Math = Fun!™

From Addition to Multiplication

by Jerry Pallotta
Illustrated by Rob Bolster

SCHOLASTIC INC.
New York   Toronto   London   Auckland   Sydney
Mexico City   New Delhi   Hong Kong   Buenos Aires

Thank you to Debbie, Jamie, Karen, Pam, and Peggy.
—Jerry Pallotta

This book is dedicated to Suzanne Galvin—a dedicated educator.
—Rob Bolster

ISBN 0-439-89635-5
12 11 10 9 8 7 6 5 4 3 2 1   6 7 8 9 10 11/0
Printed in the U.S.A.
First printing, September 2006

GET READY FOR A MATH ADVENTURE!

Let's have some fun!
We are going to climb from addition to multiplication.
Gather your climbing gear: helmet, harness,
special shoes, rope, bolts, cams, and carabiners.

MATH GEAR

We need some math equipment, too!
Make sure we have a plus sign, a multiplication sign, numbers
zero through nine, parentheses, and some graph paper.
Let's start climbing into higher math.

CLIMBING GEAR

Here is some climbing gear.
How many ropes are there?
We can find out in different ways.

COUNTING

1 2 3 4 5
6 7 8 9 10
11 12 13 14 15

Count by ones!

That took a long time!

Count the ropes.
One, two, three, four, five,
six, seven, eight, nine, ten, eleven,
twelve, thirteen, fourteen, fifteen.
When climbing, we take only one step at a time.
But there is an easier way to count the ropes.

COUNT SETS

Make groups!
Each group is
called a set.

$$5 \\ 5 \\ +5 \\ \hline 15$$

Here's a way to figure out
how many rope coils there are.
Put the ropes in sets of five,
and add!

*How many
sets are
there?*

One, two, three sets.

ADDITION

$$
\begin{array}{r}
3 \\
3 \\
3 \\
3 \\
+3 \\
\hline
15
\end{array}
$$

A plus sign adds two or more numbers together.

This is a mathematical symbol. The numbers above and below it are equal in value.

Each rope represents a number.
You can group numbers together just like ropes.
Equal groups of numbers will help you
learn addition and multiplication.
Let's add them.
Three plus three plus three plus
three plus three equals fifteen.

MULTIPLICATION

This is a multiplication sign.

It is used to multiply two or more numbers together.
The numbers being multiplied are called factors.

$$3 \times 5 = 15$$

Three times five equals fifteen.

$$5 \times 3 = 15$$

Five times three equals fifteen.

The answer in a multiplication equation is called the product.
Multiplication is a way to do repeated addition faster.
In the equations above, how many sets are there?
How many items are there in each set?

ROWS

This is a row.

There are three rows.

$$5 \times 3 = 15$$

Find a new foothold and climb to a higher concept.
Arrange the ropes in rows.
A row is side to side, or horizontal.
Each row has five ropes in it.

COLUMNS

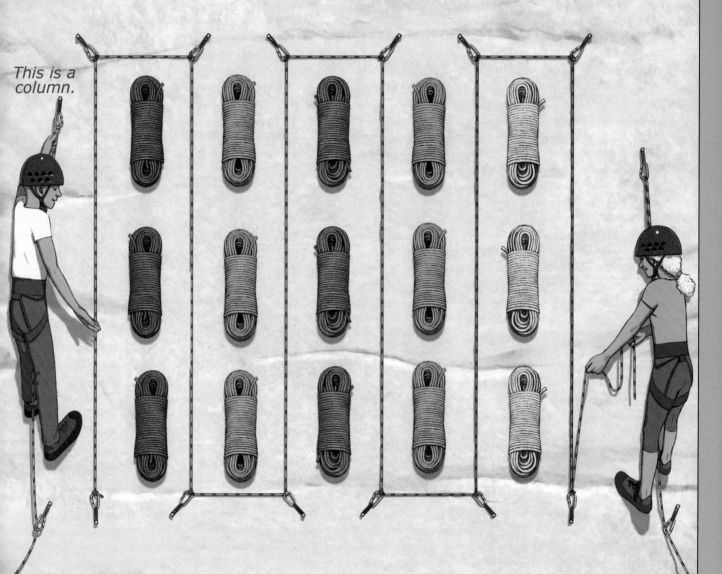

This is a column.

A column is up and down, or vertical.
The climbers are on a vertical ascent.
Each column has three ropes in it.

Learn how to make a multiplication table.
Put the numbers from zero to ten in order.
Vertically works great!

Multiplication facts take you to higher math.

0	0×1	$0 \times 1 = 0$
1	1×1	$1 \times 1 = 1$
2	2×1	$2 \times 1 = 2$
3	3×1	$3 \times 1 = 3$
4	4×1	$4 \times 1 = 4$
5	5×1	$5 \times 1 = 5$
6	6×1	$6 \times 1 = 6$
7	7×1	$7 \times 1 = 7$
8	8×1	$8 \times 1 = 8$
9	9×1	$9 \times 1 = 9$
10	10×1	$10 \times 1 = 10$

Put a multiplication sign after each
number and multiply by the number one.
You are working horizontally now.
Put equal signs next to the factors and list
the products.

A TABLE

Now follow the same steps with the number two.
Continue with the number three.

Keep going higher, all the way up to ten.

$0 \times 2 = 0$	$0 \times 3 = 0$	$0 \times 4 = 0$
$1 \times 2 = 2$	$1 \times 3 = 3$	$1 \times 4 = 4$
$2 \times 2 = 4$	$2 \times 3 = 6$	$2 \times 4 =$
$3 \times 2 = 6$	$3 \times 3 = 9$	$3 \times 4 =$
$4 \times 2 = 8$	$4 \times 3 = 12$	$4 \times 4 =$
$5 \times 2 = 10$	$5 \times 3 = 15$	$5 \times 4 =$
$6 \times 2 = 12$	$6 \times 3 = 18$	$6 \times 4 =$
$7 \times 2 = 14$	$7 \times 3 = 21$	$7 \times 4 =$
$8 \times 2 = 16$	$8 \times 3 = 24$	$8 \times 4 =$
$9 \times 2 = 18$	$9 \times 3 = 27$	$9 \times 4 =$
$10 \times 2 = 20$	$10 \times 3 = 30$	$10 \times 4 =$

This is great. I am making my own multiplication table!

MULTIPLICATION

$0 \times 1 = 0$	$0 \times 2 = 0$	$0 \times 3 = 0$	$0 \times 4 = 0$	$0 \times 5 = 0$
$1 \times 1 = 1$	$1 \times 2 = 2$	$1 \times 3 = 3$	$1 \times 4 = 4$	$1 \times 5 = 5$
$2 \times 1 = 2$	$2 \times 2 = 4$	$2 \times 3 = 6$	$2 \times 4 = 8$	$2 \times 5 = 10$
$3 \times 1 = 3$	$3 \times 2 = 6$	$3 \times 3 = 9$	$3 \times 4 = 12$	$3 \times 5 = 15$
$4 \times 1 = 4$	$4 \times 2 = 8$	$4 \times 3 = 12$	$4 \times 4 = 16$	$4 \times 5 = 20$
$5 \times 1 = 5$	$5 \times 2 = 10$	$5 \times 3 = 15$	$5 \times 4 = 20$	$5 \times 5 = 25$
$6 \times 1 = 6$	$6 \times 2 = 12$	$6 \times 3 = 18$	$6 \times 4 = 24$	$6 \times 5 = 30$
$7 \times 1 = 7$	$7 \times 2 = 14$	$7 \times 3 = 21$	$7 \times 4 = 28$	$7 \times 5 = 35$
$8 \times 1 = 8$	$8 \times 2 = 16$	$8 \times 3 = 24$	$8 \times 4 = 32$	$8 \times 5 = 40$
$9 \times 1 = 9$	$9 \times 2 = 18$	$9 \times 3 = 27$	$9 \times 4 = 36$	$9 \times 5 = 45$
$10 \times 1 = 10$	$10 \times 2 = 20$	$10 \times 3 = 30$	$10 \times 4 = 40$	$10 \times 5 = 50$

Learn your multiplication tables.
Memorize them.
Notice that in multiplication, you can reverse the
factors and still come up with the same product.
Climbing requires many skills.
Practicing your tables is also a great skill.

TABLES

$0 \times 6 = 0$	$0 \times 7 = 0$	$0 \times 8 = 0$	$0 \times 9 = 0$	$0 \times 10 = 0$
$1 \times 6 = 6$	$1 \times 7 = 7$	$1 \times 8 = 8$	$1 \times 9 = 9$	$1 \times 10 = 10$
$2 \times 6 = 12$	$2 \times 7 = 14$	$2 \times 8 = 16$	$2 \times 9 = 18$	$2 \times 10 = 20$
$3 \times 6 = 18$	$3 \times 7 = 21$	$3 \times 8 = 24$	$3 \times 9 = 27$	$3 \times 10 = 30$
$4 \times 6 = 24$	$4 \times 7 = 28$	$4 \times 8 = 32$	$4 \times 9 = 36$	$4 \times 10 = 40$
$5 \times 6 = 30$	$5 \times 7 = 35$	$5 \times 8 = 40$	$5 \times 9 = 45$	$5 \times 10 = 50$
$6 \times 6 = 36$	$6 \times 7 = 42$	$6 \times 8 = 48$	$6 \times 9 = 54$	$6 \times 10 = 60$
$7 \times 6 = 42$	$7 \times 7 = 49$	$7 \times 8 = 56$	$7 \times 9 = 63$	$7 \times 10 = 70$
$8 \times 6 = 48$	$8 \times 7 = 56$	$8 \times 8 = 64$	$8 \times 9 = 72$	$8 \times 10 = 80$
$9 \times 6 = 54$	$9 \times 7 = 63$	$9 \times 8 = 72$	$9 \times 9 = 81$	$9 \times 10 = 90$
$10 \times 6 = 60$	$10 \times 7 = 70$	$10 \times 8 = 80$	$10 \times 9 = 90$	$10 \times 10 = 100$

Being able to reverse the factors is called the commutative property of multiplication.
Numbers can commute from one place to another.
Look for patterns—there are logical patterns everywhere!
One climber leads and another follows.
They can change places at any time.
No matter who leads, they can still reach the top.

GRID

Another way to make a multiplication
table is to make a grid.
It is a shortcut.

A grid is a network of evenly spaced
horizontal and vertical lines.
It is also called a graph.

ARRAY

Now fill in the grid with numbers—
but not with random numbers!
Put one, two, three, four, five in the first vertical column
and two, three, four, five in the first horizontal row.

1	2	3	4	5
2	4	6	8	10
3	6	9	12	15
4	8	12	16	20
5	10	15	20	25

Climbing this rock wall is hard work.

But making the array of numbers was easy.

We have made an array!
The first row or column multiplies by ones,
the second row or column multiplies by twos.
This array is also a multiplication table.

GRAPH PAPER

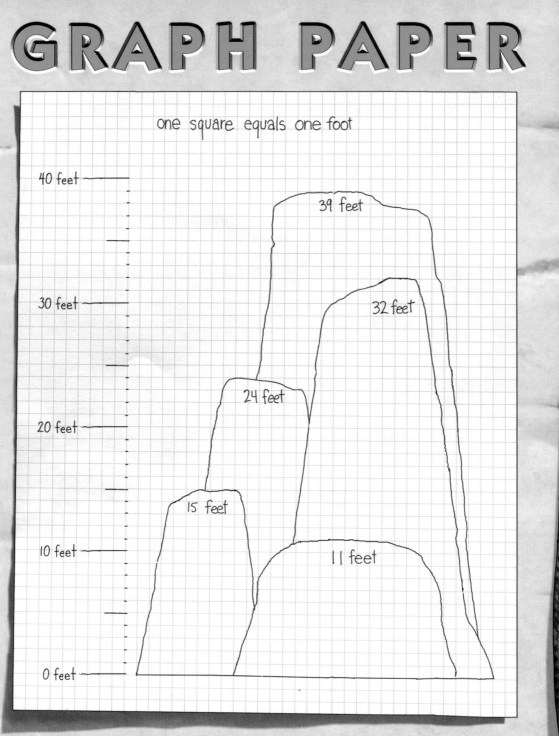

one square equals one foot

40 feet

39 feet

32 feet

30 feet

24 feet

20 feet

15 feet

10 feet

11 feet

0 feet

Making a grid is easy when you use graph paper.
Sketching out the mountain on graph paper is good, too!
Plan the climb.
How high is it to the top?
How much rope do we need?
How many bolts should we carry?
Do we have enough time to get every climber to the top safely?

ARRAY TO TEN

1	2	3	4	5	6	7	8	9	10
2	4	6	8	10	12	14	16	18	20
3	6	9	12	15	18	21	24	27	30
4	8	12	16	20	24	28	32	36	40
5	10	15	20	25	30	35	40	45	50
6	12	18	24	30	36	42	48	54	60
7	14	21	28	35	42	49	56	63	70
8	16	24	32	40	48	56	64	72	80
9	18	27	36	45	54	63	72	81	90
10	20	30	40	50	60	70	80	90	100

$$3 \times 3 = 9 \qquad 4 \times 6 = 24$$
$$8 \times 4 = 32 \qquad 10 \times 10 = 100$$

Here is a bigger array on a larger grid!
This one goes from one to ten!
Take a look and you can see how to use the base ten
array as a tool to learn multiplication facts.
Find the three on the left column and the three on the
top row and you can see that it equals nine.
Do the same with four times six; it equals twenty-four.
Eight times four equals thirty-two.
And ten times ten equals one hundred!

To go further and learn to multiply larger numbers,
it is important to understand place value.
A number's place in relation to a decimal point
determines its value.
Learn the different places: ones, tens, hundreds, thousands.
You get the idea!

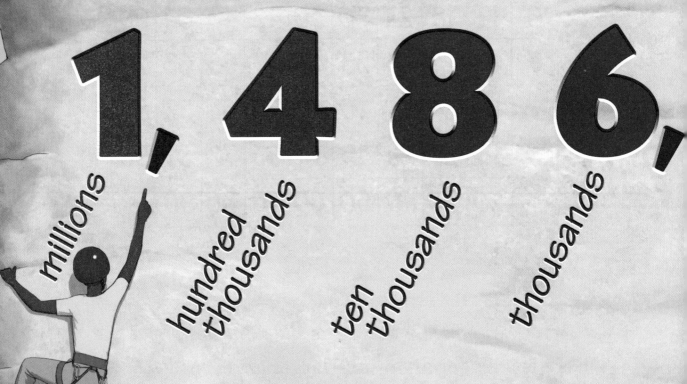

1, 4 8 6,

millions

hundred
thousands

ten
thousands

thousands

One million four hundred eighty-six thousand
nine hundred thirty-two.
Notice the commas.
It is customary to put a comma
between every three places.

VALUE

A decimal point marks the place between whole numbers and fractions of numbers.

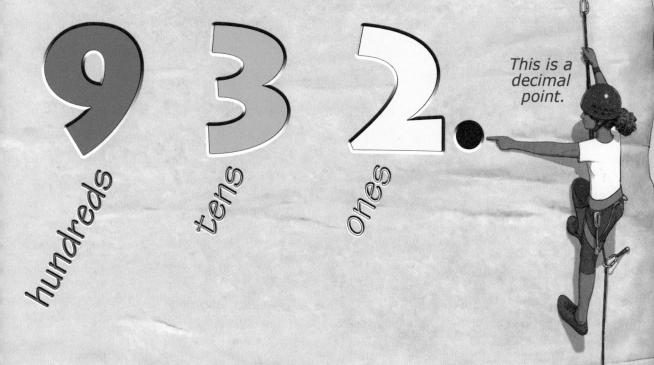

9 hundreds

3 tens

2. ones

This is a decimal point.

Numbers to the left of a decimal point are whole numbers.
Numbers to the right of a decimal point are fractions.
The millions place is seven places away from the decimal point.
Keep on climbing!

TWO DIGITS

A climber needs twenty-one bolts to get to the top safely.
Four kids are climbing to the summit.
How many bolts are needed to get all four to the top?
Twenty-one times four equals eighty-four.

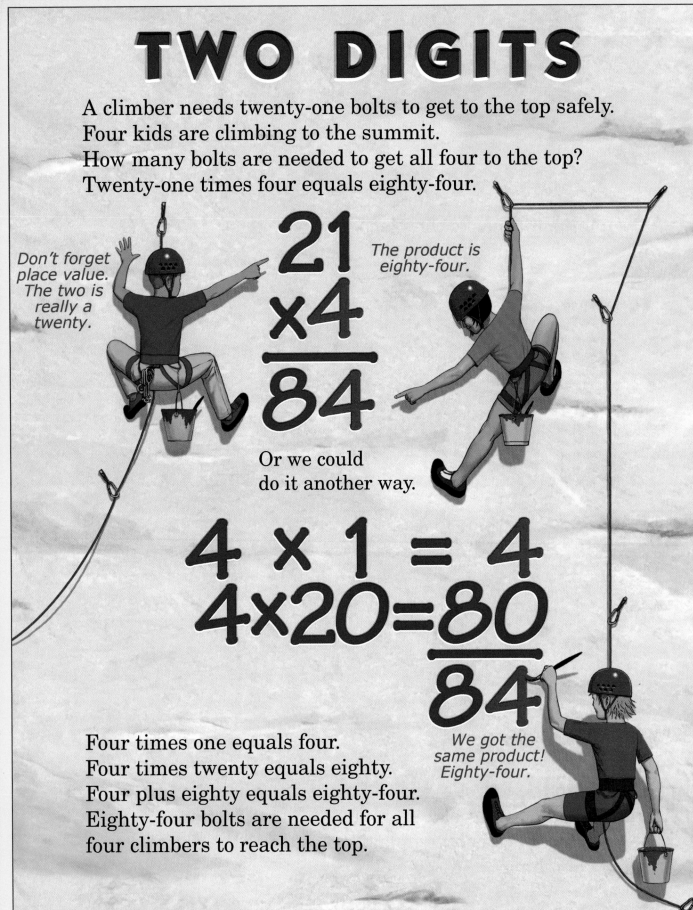

Don't forget place value. The two is really a twenty.

$$\begin{array}{r} 21 \\ \times 4 \\ \hline 84 \end{array}$$

The product is eighty-four.

Or we could
do it another way.

$$4 \times 1 = 4$$
$$4 \times 20 = 80$$
$$\overline{84}$$

Four times one equals four.
Four times twenty equals eighty.
Four plus eighty equals eighty-four.
Eighty-four bolts are needed for all
four climbers to reach the top.

We got the same product! Eighty-four.

TWO DIGITS AND CARRY

Sixty-three kids invited five friends each to climb with them. How many friends were invited climbing?

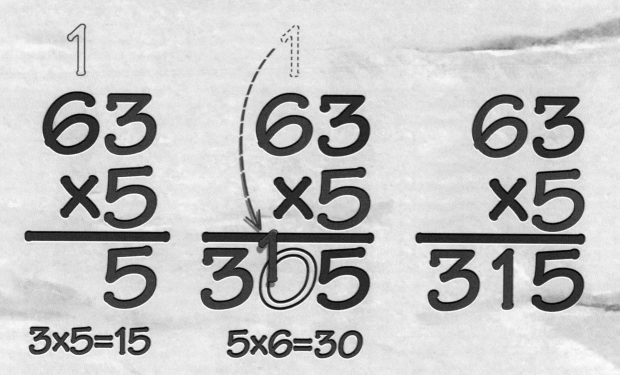

3x5=15   5x6=30

Five times three equals fifteen.
Carry the one to the tens place.
Five times six equals thirty plus the one equals thirty-one.
The product is three hundred fifteen.

Or you could do it in your head like this:

5x3=15   5x60=300

The sum of fifteen plus three hundred is three hundred fifteen.

THREE DIGITS

Each of three kids needs one hundred twenty-three
feet of rope to climb to the next section.
How much rope in total is needed?
Using multiplication can help you solve the problem.
There are a few ways you can figure this out.

$$
\begin{array}{r}
123 \\
\times 3 \\
\hline
369
\end{array}
$$

One hundred twenty-three times three
equals three hundred sixty-nine.

Think! Here is another way.
Three times three equals nine.
Three times twenty equals sixty.
Three times one hundred equals three hundred.
Add the products.

We get the same answer:

$$
\begin{array}{r}
9 \\
60 \\
+300 \\
\hline
\text{total} = 369
\end{array}
$$

THREE DIGITS AND CARRY

Six hundred forty-two kids climbed on the wall this year.
Each climber had eight carabiners.
How many carabiners in total did they have?

Carry the three to the hundreds column.

Carry the one to the tens column.

$$
\begin{array}{r}
3 \\
6\,4\,2 \\
\times\ \ \ 8 \\
\hline
5{,}136
\end{array}
$$

Eight times two is sixteen, carry the one to the tens place.
Eight times four equals thirty-two, plus one is thirty-three.
Carry the three to the hundreds place.
Eight times six equals forty-eight, plus three equals fifty-one.
The product is five thousand one hundred thirty-six.

Or, you can solve
the problem like this:

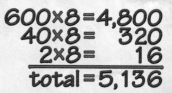

$$
\begin{array}{rr}
600\times8= & 4{,}800 \\
40\times8= & 320 \\
2\times8= & 16 \\
\hline
\text{total}= & 5{,}136
\end{array}
$$

FOUR DIGITS

Four thousand thirty-one climbers have signed up to climb next year. Each climber has two coils of rope. How many coils of rope will there be in total?

This three is really thirty.

This four is really four thousand.

$$\begin{array}{r} 4{,}031 \\ \times\ 2 \\ \hline 8{,}062 \end{array}$$

Two times one equals two.
Two times three equals six.
Two times zero equals zero.
Two times four equals eight.

8,062

The zero is holding the place, but there are no hundreds in the hundreds place.

FOUR DIGITS AND CARRY

This three represents three thousand!

This is four hundred. We added another hundred.

$$\begin{array}{r} \overset{2}{}\overset{1}{} \\ 3,421 \\ \times 6 \\ \hline 20,526 \end{array}$$

There are three thousand four hundred twenty-one climbers in a rock-climbing club.

They each own six rock-climbing books.

What is the total of all the rock-climbing books they own?

The product is twenty thousand five hundred twenty-six!

Six times one is six.

Six times two is twelve, carry the one to the hundreds place.

Six times four is twenty-four, plus one is twenty-five.

Carry the two to the thousands place.

Six times three is eighteen, plus two is twenty.

The answer is twenty thousand five hundred twenty-six.

That's a lot of books!

THREE FACTORS

Two kids climbed to the top of five mountains every day for seven days.
How many times were the mountains climbed?

$$2 \times 5 \times 7 = ?$$

Two times five times seven equals what?
Now we are multiplying three factors.

Oh, no! Now what do we do?

Let's think . . . I know! We need parentheses.

PARENTHESES

Put parentheses around the two and the five.
Multiply them first.
Two times five equals ten.
Now multiply ten times seven.
Ten times seven equals seventy!

$$(2×5)×7=$$

We made mini-equations.

$$10 × 7 =$$

$$10 × 7 = 70$$

Using parentheses is awesome!

Or we could have multiplied five times seven first.
Five times seven equals thirty-five.
Thirty-five times two equals seventy.

FOUR FACTORS

Two climbers climbed three mountains.
They did this every day for four days.
Every time they climbed a mountain,
they each used five new ropes.
How many new ropes did the climbers use?

$$2 \times 3 \times 4 \times 5 =$$

*Wow!
Four factors!*

*If we think,
we can do it!*

PARENTHESES

$$(2 \times 3) \times (4 \times 5) =$$

Use parentheses!

$$6 \times 20 =$$

$$6 \times 20 = 120$$

Two times three equals six.
Four times five equals twenty.
Six times twenty equals one hundred twenty!
In multiplication, it does not matter what
order you multiply the factors.

THE SUMMIT

We made it to the summit!
We traveled from addition to multiplication!